THE BIRD WHO SANG AGAIN

Rediscover Your God-Given Voice

Judy Moore

Copyright © Judy Moore, 2021

Published 2021 by Waverley Abbey Resources, a trading name of CWR,
Waverley Abbey House, Waverley Lane, Farnham, Surrey GU9 8EP, UK.
Registered Charity No. 294387. Registered limited company No. 1990308.

The right of Judy Moore to be identified as the author of this work has been
asserted by her in accordance with the Copyright, Designs and Patents Act 1988,
sections 77 and 78.

For a list of National Distributors, visit waverleyabbeyresources.org/distributors

Concept development and editing by Waverley Abbey Resources.

Design and production by Waverley Abbey Resources.

Printed in the UK by Page Bros.

ISBN: 978-1-78951-269-4

This book is dedicated to my Dad
who finally lost his voice, but
never lost his song!

I am so grateful to Judy for writing this imaginative book. Each chapter encourages you to sing your own distinctive song, even in the middle of life's noisy demands. Each story is a beautiful invitation to shelter under God's wings and to consider his faithfulness again - I highly recommend it.

Cathy Madavan

Speaker, writer, broadcaster and author of
Irrepressible and *Digging for Diamonds*

I loved this book and it spoke to me very deeply. Entertaining, deep, wise, fun, insightful yet easy to read, warm and hugely challenging, are all words I'd use to describe Judy Moore's latest book. It is a wonderful cocktail of life discovery for those searching for greater depth, fulfilment, kindness and acceptance as they pursue their life journey.

Jill Garrett

Leadership coach and personality
strengths consultant worldwide

Using her considerable experience and bright humour,
Judy guides us gently from the wings and then coaxes us to sing our own song boldly and proudly from centre stage.
All the right notes and all in the right order.

David Robinson and Michael Taylorson

Searchlight Theatre Company

Contents

Foreword

It was the late Walt Disney, the chap famous for the mouse and those magic kingdoms, who tells of his discovery of a type of person he describes as a *life enhancer*. These beautiful souls are quick to reach out and live with their eyes and hearts open. Fuelled by a passion to strengthen and enrich others, the life enhancers encourage, lift up and inspire.

They are founts of joy; human sunrises. If you know a life enhancer, hold on to them tightly, because they are rare and priceless. Their presence in our lives lifts our hearts, puts a spring in our step and keeps us going when the weather is bleak and blustery.

Judy Moore is a life enhancer. Her face very naturally forms a beautiful smile that radiates warmth. She is very good at public speaking, but when it comes to care, she does a lot more than talk. She has weathered her own stormy seasons but has navigated them with grit. She's a very gifted actor, too. And then she writes with wit and charm, inviting us to joy rather than bullying us to buck up and sport a false grin. Her passion for life bleeds beautifully through the sentences that follow in this book. In calling us to a life of song, she's no stern, silent choir leader, but rather welcomes us to join her in the melody.

How do I know all this? My wife, Kay, and I have been privileged to spend weeks – literally – on the road with Judy, as we've trundled around the UK to perform evenings of theatre, storytelling and music. When you spend a lot of time in a relatively uncomfortable transit van, you get to see a person up close and personal. Ms Moore is the real deal.

So, get ready to have your heart warmed, your mind challenged and your day brightened, because this book, I'm sure, will help us all to sing.

Jeff Lucas

Introduction

> 'Once upon a time... there was the simple understanding that to sing at dawn and to sing at dusk was to heal the world through joy. The birds still remember what we have forgotten, that the world is meant to be celebrated'
> Terry Tempest Williams

Perhaps every life – yours and mine – is a song to the world. Each song can be very different indeed. The incredible miracle of the human spirit is that a unique, unmatched, unequalled song exudes from within us, sometimes wordless, sometimes beautifully written, sometimes malevolent... and we are changing our atmosphere every day, singing to ourselves and those around us, our listeners.

A song can be made up of light and shade, pauses and pace, beauty and pain, torment and joy. So too with us. A song is written to say something, every song has a meaning and a purpose, and our lives are the same.

Now and then songwriters get into trouble for plagiarism, both knowingly and unknowingly copying other people's work. The same, I believe is true of us. Sometimes there is a real instinct to copy others, to

sing someone else's song rather than our own.
My hope is that we will celebrate all that is unique
for us to be and all the original notes and words that
make up our own discovered song of life. If we are to
plagiarise or copy, I believe that Jesus' life is the one,
above all others, that is worth copying. His words and
actions are the ones that we were created to copy in
order to enhance and beautify the very essence, the
very soul of our song.

I am not a fan of birds, indeed those of you who
know me know that I have an inherited phobia of
them that hasn't yet gone away. The irony of me
writing a book with a bird in the title is not lost on me!
I do believe, however, that they have much to teach us.

There are nearly three hundred references to birds
in the Bible. Clearly, they have something to say
(or sing!) about life and faith. Jesus uses the sparrow
to emphasise one of the most beautiful lessons: God's
incredible love, care and attention for each of us.
The smallest and plainest bird, worth next to nothing
commercially, and yet the Father's eye is always on it
(see Matthew 10:29).

But what of the song of birds? How do they even
know what to sing? Do they rehearse? How do they
know the right notes to attract a mate, to warn a fellow
feathered friend, to herald a new dawn? And what if,
suddenly, one forgot the words, the notes, what if a
bird suddenly lost its song, or worse, never found it?

In recent months, scientists have reported that a rare songbird known as the honeyeater, once abundant in south-eastern Australia, has become so threatened it has started to lose its song. It is now listed as critically endangered with only approximately three hundred individual birds remaining. Dr Ross Crates, a researcher with the Difficult Bird Research Group, discovered that each individual isolated bird was found to be singing a really weird song. In fact, he goes on to say they sounded like an entirely different species or could barely sing at all. Songbirds learn their songs from each other's song in the very same way that we learn to speak from those around us. As part of the ongoing research, birdsong of the species is being played to the individual honeyeater birds so that they recapture their song and begin to sing again as only their species can sing! If this doesn't happen they are at risk of complete extinction as they need their own unique song to attract a suitable mate and continue the honeyeater line. If we are to stay true to our own unique song we need each other and we need to listen to each other's song sufficiently to discover the joy of who we are.

In this time as we emerge from a global pandemic when many of us have been left very isolated and perhaps have struggled to remember our song, my hope is that we will draw closer still to one another, building ever stronger communities so that no one

forgets what their unique voice sounds like.
We haven't been allowed to sing in our places of
worship for over a year in order to curb the spread
of the coronavirus and have been reduced to strange,
muted humming from behind our masks. May each
of us learn to sing again with all our hearts and to
be grateful for that unmuted, unmasked freedom
once again. May our songs ring out to encourage
one another with the overtones of love and delight
attracting others to the unique love song of God for
His people.

As you begin this book, I wonder how your song
is? Do you feel like you have lost your purpose, that
life has lost meaning, that your actions and words are
unheard and unseen? My hope and my prayer as I
write this book is to inspire you and your life to sing
out, to change and impact your surroundings, to tell
the story you have been uniquely crafted to tell.

With each chapter comes stories, some teaching and
some lessons learned about how we sing to the world
around us. Storytelling is the primary way that Jesus
taught and inspired, using humour and everyday life
to engage His listeners. The stories you will read here
are sometimes light hearted and some may seem trivial,
others are far from it. They are retold, nevertheless,
in the hope and belief that you might relate to and be
entertained by them as well as perhaps gleaning truth
and encouragement from the Bible to enrich 'your song'.

As a person of faith, with belief in Jesus and the truth of His message, I will be referencing my faith throughout the book. Please read on, even if you do not share that faith, as I would love your life to find its unique song and for you to know that every life in the world sings with significance and purpose!

ONE

A FEAR
OF BIRDS

'One generation shall commend your works to another, and shall declare your mighty acts'
Psalm 145:4, ESV

'And what you have heard from me in the presence of many witnesses entrust to faithful men, who will be able to teach others also.'
2 Timothy 2:2, ESV

The irony of writing a book with 'bird' in the title is that I have a deep-rooted fear of birds. It is a phobia and more common than you might think. My rational self knows that birds have much to teach us; that they get a good press in the Bible. For one, they are loved and cared for by God and precious to Him. So then, what twisted part of me wishes God had never thought up birds in the first place? Why do I wince or fall to the ground dramatically when a sparrow flexes his wingspan in my direction? Well, maybe not a sparrow but definitely a pigeon!

The answer is... my mum. Isn't it always, as Freud would say? But seriously in this case it is true. Through no fault of her own, my mum had a crippling phobia of birds.

Once, when she was just a baby, she was lying in a pram outside a shop (that was back in the day when people left prams unattended outside shops!) and a large crow landed on the pram and flapped over her terrorising her. She screamed and screamed until her mum, my grandma, ran out of the shop and shooed the offending creature away.

Fast forward thirty years and I must say she did an amazing job being a mum to two daughters. And yet many a family picnic would commence with my dad shooing and flapping, clearing the way to be bird-free before the picnic could begin! Many a shopping trip would be interrupted by Mum pulling both us girls down to the ground much like, I imagine, parents must have done in the war when fighter planes came overhead – only in our case it was a pigeon or a seagull! On one occasion, when a rogue bird came down the chimney, all I remember is mass panic and mass evacuation of our home. In short, I watched and learned. Birds were the enemy, to be feared and removed from any domestic scene.

Living with this inherited fear, I have been in some situations where the presence or appearance of birds has led to some really compulsive, dramatic and irrational behaviour.

Working for a season in a lovely sedate bookshop in Kingston Upon Thames, imagine a scene of quiet and polite service, a lady innocently buying her latest paperback, when suddenly I start screaming and shouting for help, dropping the change and running out of the shop leaving the till open! I remember to this day the swoop of the pigeon brushing across my head as he flew toward the self-help section (I might have embellished the pigeon's choice of book...).

Another scene and street theatre begins in a lovely Welsh town... enter jackdaw stage left. Suddenly the actress (me in case you were wondering) drops dramatically to the ground and spends the scene swerving about in an attempt to deliver lines with credibility while being joined by Jack, the local Jackdaw, known to many locals, who clearly had a bit of a flair for open air theatre.

So just two examples of how this learned fear has manifested itself in my life. Friends and family over the years have become used to me grabbing them and pulling them down while a pigeon looms above us. Drinking or dining alfresco is a challenge and has led to some very embarrassing reactions to sparrows and seagulls alike as they join us at the table for a halloumi wrap or a skinny flat white.

Whether we are parents or not there are those who come after us who will learn our song. The song of our life outlives us. Some of our favourite songs are classics – the writers of which are now long gone. As we gauge and navigate our purpose in life, we can be reassured that our life lives on, that we each pass on a legacy of meaning and impact.

As you read this chapter it may be helpful to reflect on what your classic song will be. How will you be remembered, what legacy will you leave behind?

As you will see from the two scripture references at the start of this chapter, the Bible recognises generational learning and legacy. The very nature of the Christian faith is to mimic its founder. In fact, Christian means *little Christ*, the goal being to copy, to emulate, to learn from Jesus and pass it on. Even the word 'gospel' in the original Greek means 'an announcement of good news'. It is not just that we have the good news that we can be free from sin and death, but we announce it and pass it on to others because it's so good.

I'm often challenged and motivated by the idea that someone I care about might finally find the joy of Jesus right at the end of life and turn to me and say: *Why didn't you let me know about this before? I could have lived such a different life.*

A few months ago, I was privileged to participate in something called The Life Plan, produced by the Patterson Organisation. As a result of time receiving coaching and reflecting on life, you are enabled to produce your 'life purpose' statement. Here is what we came up with for me: 'I will be a woman of a free and light spirit, extending the table of celebration, living and telling the story of Jesus, excelling in love.'

The idea of this process is that you check in with the statement on a regular basis to see how you are living it out. You create a statement with God's help that summarises what you would love to be true of your life when you're gone and receive from your life while you are living it. In other words, it helps your life's song to keep on being sung in line with your values and your heart. I'm no musician but I guess it's almost as if you have a line of the melody to sing by and the rest is like jamming around that theme.

Alfred Nobel famously got a newspaper through his door one day that mistakenly reported his own death. Once he had regained his composure at this shocking mistake, he read on, curious to hear what was said of his life. The headline was 'Dynamite king died. He was the merchant of death.' (Not what any of us would wish for as a life purpose statement I suspect.) As the inventor of dynamite, of course, this was in some way true, but he asked himself: *Is this how I will be remembered?* From that day onward, he decided to work toward peace and his name is now synonymous with the award given for outstanding contribution towards peace. Conviction and revelation changed his life song completely. He is remembered for peace and life, not destruction and death.

So, as we close this chapter, let's reflect on what our song will be.

My mum may have taught me an irrational fear of birds, but she also taught me open-hearted hospitality, generosity and excelling in love – all of which you will see in my life purpose statement. The beautiful song of her life has shaped mine.

> He put a new song in my mouth, a hymn of praise to our God. Many will see and fear the LORD and put their trust in him. (Psalm 40:3)

SING
A LITTLE
LOUDER

'Sing a little louder…

My weapon is a melody…

I will watch the darkness flee…'
Raise a Hallelujah, Bethel Music

'The light shines in the darkness, and the darkness has not overcome it' John 1:5

'For me, to sing is like when you go to war'
Helen Berhane

Barbed wire and brightly coloured ribbons form a beautifully poignant picture of hope and faith laced with deep pain. I'm standing at the border between North and South Korea. Every coloured ribbon here has been lovingly tied on to the barbed wire fence by someone to represent a loved one still in North Korea;

a sign that they believe they will one day be free. One ribbon for one life, one song on mute that they pray will one day be heard.

I find this picture such a powerful reminder of our lives: of pain laced with hope, of holding on in the face of total despair.

Looking out over the beauty of the mountains through the lens of a telescope, I'm as close as I can legally be to North Korea. It's a land where people are taught to use the word love only for their leader. I can't see any people, only a lone tractor ploughing a faded field. We are here to find stories, to meet those who are free, to hear their heart for those who remain.

Basing ourselves in Seoul in South Korea, we are to meet women of incredible courage. Women who have swum through the ice-cold sea to China, who have carried their children through snow drifts, who now open up their underground homes to cook us rice and vegetables. My time here is teaching me a great deal about courage and faith winning through against all human odds, and about the power of refusing to let your hope be extinguished. We were greeted with the power of heartfelt song on the day we arrived. Men and women alike, these students who escaped from North Korea, learning to love, learning to heal, sang with all their heart and soul to welcome us. I'm already tearful and overwhelmed. There is so much joy here and yet so much pain. Many are estranged from family, waiting still for reconciliation. But they have discovered faith in Jesus, and it has brought them the most incredible freedom. God spoke to them and they followed His light. One lady tells me she heard an audible voice while she was washing clothes in a mountain stream. The voice told her she was *loved*, a word familiar only to her as a political term of allegiance. Who would ever address such a controversial statement to her? Years later she read almost the very same words in the pages of a New Testament Bible.

It is such an enormous privilege to work with these students, many brand-new disciples of Jesus, who are so hungry for the truth. We spent one day exploring the word love and reclaiming it from all their previous indoctrination. We also found out just how much we had in common with our addiction to technology and smart phones, our resistance to being still, our compulsion to stay busy. We could see how clearly we were just the same yet so incredibly different. The same plants at root yet placed and nurtured in completely contrasting soil.

One thing is now very clear to me. When your song has been muted and supressed for so long, when you do find your voice again, there seems to be so much joy, so much wonder and gratitude for the sheer freedom to sing with all your soul!

The persecuted church is a mystery to many of us in the West. Why, for example, in the book *Tortured for Christ*, does Richard Wurmbrand find himself with the urge to dance with joy when his feet are in chains and he exists in solitary confinement year after year? Is it perhaps that, when all is stripped away and we have nowhere else to turn, the joy of the Lord is truly our strength and our song?

In the New Testament, in the book of Acts, chapter 16, we hear a similar story. Paul and Silas are in prison simply because they have prayed for the freedom of a slave girl. The authorities see them as a threat and try to silence them by putting them in prison. What happens next is truly amazing. They start to sing hymns of praise to God and an earthquake occurs that shakes the whole prison and leads miraculously to their release. Even their jailor is so impacted that he, and finally his whole family, come to faith in Jesus. When we witness faith like this, faith that sings loudly in the darkness, faith that finds something to be thankful for in the middle of the mess and pain of life, we can't help but be challenged.

Helen Berhane is a gospel singer who was once imprisoned for her faith and placed in a freezing cold metal container in Eritrea. In that place of utter dark despair and sheer injustice she chooses to sing. She tells us that, as she sang, the Holy Spirit covered all the pain she had. She even issues a challenge to those of us who live in plenty and freedom to keep our song alive.

Praise is a powerful weapon. It can lift our eyes to a different horizon beyond the one we can see with human eyes. C.S. Lewis states 'praise almost seems to be inner health made audible'.[1]

Augustine says that, because of sin, we misidentify what makes us happy. We attach happiness to circumstances staying pleasurable and meeting our perceived needs. Yet the wonder of those amid persecution is that they have learned to sing a new song. They have learned to sing in order to watch the darkness flee as the song goes.

So, what about us? Why might we find that our song is muted or is fading fast? We live in the West amidst fear, distraction and anxiety. We breathe the air of consumerism and self-love. We learn to grab, to take, to have, whereas many in other lands have learned the secret to giving away their last piece of bread and still being joyful.

I don't remember a great deal of my early days in the church my family were part of growing up, but I do remember one class that was led by a deacon called Sister Lois. She taught us that *praise is a sacrifice*. I have absolutely no idea why that is the thing I most remember but it has always stayed with me.

I truly believe that in this life we will have trials of many kinds – as Peter tells us in 1 Peter 1:6 – but that these trials will refine and add strength to our song in incredible ways. The soul who has learned to sing in the darkest of times will inspire so many others to sing a little louder.

Does my faith look big in this?

> 'To thine own self be true' William Shakespeare

> 'Look at the birds of the air; they do not sow or reap or store away in barns, and yet your heavenly Father feeds them... See how the flowers of the field grow. They do not labour or spin. Yet I tell you that not even Solomon in all his splendour was dressed like one of these' Matthew 6:26,28–29

One thing that birds do is let God chose their outfit. As far as we know (with the exception of the magpie) they are not known for being materialistic consumers.

I remember in my early teens, a lady came to visit the church youth group to share, with great joy, how God helped her shop for clothes and pick the outfit she was wearing. I decided at that moment (rather judgmentally) that maybe God and I had very different taste in clothes!

I am a big fan of clothes. They affect my confidence, my mood, and I really enjoy shopping for them. However, I began the year 2020 with a commitment to fast from buying any clothes for a year, and within two months, two shops in Kingston, my favourite place to shop, had already shut down! Some of my friends and family felt the two might be linked – how cheeky! I'm really not that bad...

Costume is a huge part of theatre and often plays a key role both in the exploration of character and establishing context. I once played sixteen characters within one production, which resulted in me running on stage once in a strange amalgam of two different costumes and characters. The actor I joined in the scene whispered, 'Oh Velma, I wasn't expecting to see you, if indeed it is really you!'

I have played a lizard in a production of C.S. Lewis' *The Great Divorce*, wearing a spray-on catsuit inherited from the previous actress who was about 5ft 10 and size 8 at the most! Trying to fit her costume was tricky enough, but harder still was trying to fulfil all the acrobatic movements of the lizard while squeezed into the costume so compactly.

If you have read my first book, *The Dog Who Thought His Name Was No*, you may remember that I also made a hasty two-minute appearance as Obi-Wan Kenobi in a cloak meant for a 6ft male actor. The huge hood totally swamped my 5ft 2 frame and obscured my vision completely, culminating in me blindly taking the wrong exit, walking off stage, not into the dressing room, but straight into the car park via the fire exit!

One final onstage clothes mishap to share – in a production of *The Boyfriend*, the tassels on my flapper dress caught on the button of one of the male actors' blazers and we ended up dancing very closely while my dress started to come loose every time he moved! The particular dance number was called 'There's Safety in Numbers' and that was certainly true as he heroically spared my blushes by continuing to cover me!

***

I love *The Message* version of Matthew 11:28–30 where we read that Jesus promises: 'I won't lay anything ill-fitting on you.' This seems so apt for a chapter looking at clothes and costumes. Jesus Himself is saying, *I am the greatest tailor, I know your shape, I know your fit.*

In the Old Testament, when David was about to meet Goliath, he was given borrowed armour. He was wearing someone else's ill-fitting costume. David is young and small, swamped by the armour not designed for him to wear.

Many of us, especially those like me who are the youngest sibling, grew up wearing some hand-me-downs. This is of course a really wise and prudent thing to do as parents make the best of what they have, but perhaps it is an outer sign that can mirror something deeper going on within us.

Sometimes life can take a wrong turn and become about trying to fit someone else's costumes, dressing in clothes that were hand-picked to suit someone else's shape and calling. Maybe we feel a pressure to measure up, to fill the shoes of others in our family and communities. Have you ever had things spoken over you that may have made you 'wear the wrong clothes'?

'If only you were more like your brother.'
'We thought your grades would be higher.'
'We hoped you would be married by now.'
'Is that a real job?'
And so it goes on...

In this story in the Bible, David practically calls out: *This hand-me-down costume doesn't fit me!* I wonder how many times in life we need to join David in his heartfelt cry and call out: 'This doesn't fit me!'

We can become so clothed in other people's expectations for us, their handed down desires and dreams for us, but in following Jesus and His teachings, we have a wonderful way of wearing something brand new and totally fit for purpose: His purpose for our lives.

Any birdwatcher will tell you that when a bird finds its song it can be uniquely identified. A bird is known by its song, but each one of a certain type of bird has its own different inflection, volume and register. David not only refutes what is thrust upon him, but also draws on his own unique shape, as it were. He knows what to wear and what to use and what simple weapons will work here, because of his unique life experience in using shepherd-boy weaponry.

> You come against me with sword and spear and javelin, but I come against you in the name of the LORD Almighty, the God of the armies of Israel
> (1 Samuel 17:45)

With his sling and five stones, David defeats his giant by being true to himself and true to the power of God to use him in a totally tailored and unique way.

Your DNA and fingerprint are 100% unique, crafted by your maker for you to make *your own* mark, not someone else's. One of our dangers may be that we end our days realising that we lived someone else's life, in a borrowed ill-fitting costume.

The best costume designers I have worked with are all about getting to know you first and looking at how you fit into the overall piece of theatre. They ask you questions like...

'Does this suit your shape?'
'Have you got room to move freely?'
'Would you like to have a slightly closer fit?'

The best designers want to know you first, as you really are.

The Bible brilliantly reassures us that God will give us new clothes to wear, and I believe that they are an exact match for the personality and plan He already has designed for us. Thinking back to where we began, with the earnest lady telling my youth group that God picked her outfit, it seems, at least metaphorically anyway, that perhaps she had it right!

In closing, it's worth remembering that the apostle Paul, in his letter to the church in Colossae, lists some brilliant things we can all wear:

Therefore, as Gods chosen people, holy and dearly loved, clothe yourselves with compassion, kindness, humility, gentleness and patience...
And over all these virtues put on love
(Colossians 3:12,14)

Well, that is certainly an outfit we can all agree to wear!

HOLD THE CURTAIN

'This was a divine tearing, God's way of showing that the way to His presence was now open to sinners!' Mike McKinley

'At that moment the curtain of the temple was torn in two from top to bottom. The earth shook, the rocks split.' Matthew 27:51

The curtain is both a spiritual and a theatrical symbol.

So, what a good idea it would be, I hear you say, to combine those two contexts. To use a theatre curtain to represent the curtain in the Temple that was torn in two as Jesus died, would seem like a straightforward plan...

It was a Good Friday reflective service, one of my favourite services of the year. We were meeting in the local school hall where we meet each week for one of our Sunday gatherings. I decided to make the area behind the theatre curtain the place where the cross would be positioned, hidden from view, surrounded by lilies representing death and uplights representing life and hope.

The key point in the reading where Jesus dies and breathes his last breath would be the moment of the big reveal. The curtain would swing open and we would take in a picture of the cross surrounded by signs of hope among death.

Keith, our wonderful all-round hero, in charge of facilities and Sunday operations, was on curtain-pulling duty and was waiting for the cue 'It is finished' to reveal the cross surrounded by beauty and light.

I'm not sure at what point the crucifixion story first took on the smell of smoke. I had anticipated the aroma of lilies being a key factor in the cross and its revelation, but this smoke was certainly not part of the plan!

Church and theatre can also share a sense of the audience or congregation reading significance into both the intentional and the unintentional things that go on and indeed, especially in theatre, that has saved us on many occasions, where people read a subtext into something that was never meant to happen. I'm sure there were a few members of our gathered church who started to wonder about the significance of the billowing smoke beginning to escape from beneath the heavy drapes!

'It is finished' cried the reader, and Keith's moment came, accompanied by wonderful music. The curtains parted, the cross was indeed revealed, with smoke swirling ominously around its base as lilies and paper began to smoulder thanks to the uplights being rather too close, causing them to burn. Ever the hero, Keith moved quickly with water close by, putting out whatever was almost aflame, and removing all the uplights from their sockets!

Was this an early appearance of a gardener, a disciple wracked with grief throwing water at the foot of the cross, or some other stranger? I'm sure our visitors may have pondered the identity of the man in the shadows of the cross but to those who know him they will have just concluded it was our beloved Keith serving as always, keeping everyone safe. He really is one of my heroes, so this is a lovely opportunity to honour him.

To this day, there could perhaps be those that think the smoke represented the earthquake or death breathing its last, but I shudder to think what might have happened if 'It is finished' had come any later in the story!

***

The curtain in the Temple guarded the holy of holies, the place where God's presence dwelt. The only person allowed to enter in was the high priest.

One of my favourite pieces of evidence for Jesus being truly God is this moment in history, when the curtain of the Temple is torn from top to bottom at the very moment of Jesus' death. The curtain was 30ft wide by 30ft high and an inch thick, and yet it rips *downwards*, beyond man's human reach, it rips from heaven to earth.

There are three contexts in which people of Jesus' time would have been familiar with His words 'It is finished' (or *tetelestai* in the Greek). It was a term used in business to say, 'the debt is paid'; in criminal law to say, 'a sentence had been served'; and finally it was known to be a military term to mean 'the battle is declared as won'. I just love how all these things fit together in the story. Jesus dies saying, *I've gone through with it for you and your debt is paid, your sentence is served, and the battle over death is won!*

The message of sacrifice associated with the curtain was clear to all those around Jesus. For thousands of years it had been the place of sacrifice and atonement. The place where blood sacrifices were left. The high priest would mix the blood of a goat and the blood of a bull and put it on the altar outside the holy of holies to cleanse it from the sins of the people. So, the incredible fact that the curtain rips as Jesus dies is an outward symbol of His death to finally, once and for all, pay the price for all our sins.

Now sin is a tricky word and, for some of you, it might not be one that you relate to, especially if you're exploring faith for the first time. I believe, simply put, sin is and always has been *the things we do and say that cause separation between us and a Holy God*. So, what better way for God to throw His arms open again, to say *you are welcomed in by accepting that this death is for your freedom and forgiveness*. Because of the cross, we can worship

God, we can know Him close to us wherever we are, on a beach, in a cathedral, in a tent, on a bus.

So, what of our song as we end this chapter? A bird sings on instinct, it comes from within. Birds don't rehearse (to the best of our knowledge), they sing because it is something they were made instinctively to do. Believe it or not, so were we. Each of us was created to worship – as I once read: *higher than the mind even is the human spirit.*

Saint Augustine said: 'You have made us for yourself, O Lord, and our heart is restless until it rests in you.'

Worship and work are what we are designed for, and I believe our song is a glorious combination of the two. Because the curtain was torn, because Jesus died and beat death, you and I can sing, sing with all our heart, and worship as those who have rediscovered a song, a voice, a significance, a life beyond this one. Our song is both external and internal. It rises up again every time we remember we are those who are welcomed in as the curtain opens wide.

So, friends, we can now – without hesitation – walk right up to God, into "the Holy place." Jesus has cleared the way by the blood of his sacrifice, acting as our priest before God.
(Hebrews 10:19–20, *The Message*)

WHAT IF WE FORGET THE WORDS?

'We shall come one day to a heaven where we shall gratefully know that God's great refusals were sometimes the true answers to our truest prayers.' P.T. Forsyth

'Now go; I will help you speak and will teach you what to say... [Aaron] will speak to the people for you, and it will be as if he were your mouth and as if you were God to him.' Exodus 4:12,16

As a touring actress, working on a whole variety of productions over the years, there are those inevitable moments of sheer panic when your mind goes blank, your mouth goes dry and you have totally forgotten your words. For me the worst, most memorable occasion was a long-awaited press show in America of a new play called *Skin Deep*. It had been billed as controversial in its treatment of the Church's relationship to politics and identity, and my character, Emma, was to be the mouthpiece for the most controversial speech of the production.

The first shows in the UK had gone well and no sudden loss of words had taken place. However, on arriving in the US, we were suddenly given some very late changes to our lines due to cultural relevance and interpretation. I guess for singers and actors alike, there is a hidden place in our subconscious where the words hide until we need them. Repetition and rehearsal embed these words and we can be fairly confident that we can reach them. However, when sudden changes occur, we get confused as the old version comes so readily to mind, superseding the newer version and our mind goes totally blank.

A sharp intake of breath at the start of the controversial monologue and... nothing. The old and new versions warring with each other in my mind and still nothing... when does a dramatic pause become an uncomfortable silence?

The audience look back at me, wide eyed, expectant. My throat is dry, my heart is racing and still nothing.

Certain things flash through your mind at times like this: your contract, the director's face, your dog's empty food bowl, your bank balance, your breakfast...

Suddenly a voice from the darkness shouts into the abyss of awkward silence. 'Sorry we are back early Ems, you okay?' My wonderful fellow actors, Tim and Steve, bound onto the stage to my rescue. They are the ones who know, they are the ones who feel and share my panic and they show up at the eleventh hour! Instinct and compassion lead them to enter stage left almost a scene early so I'm not left alone to die a public stage death and to end my short-lived career in spectacular fashion.

We head onward into the next scene and the next, with me giving it everything almost like never before. As soon as the curtain fell (as they say) I escaped to my dressing room with the intention of hiding there forever and secretly booking my flight home. After an extended period of tears, self-flagellation and shame I hear another voice, this time that of the director shouting from outside: 'Judy, I need to speak to you, please come out soon.'

So, this is the moment, the firing, a whole scene missed out, a situation only saved by my wonderful fellow actors, what hope was there of anything else?

'I just wanted to say well done,' he calls, 'that's the best you have ever done it. Everyone loved it, why have you been hiding all this time?'

I can't remember his exact words, when I finally tearfully emerged (this was now a really long time ago) but the gist of it was that everything had led to the best possible response. Even the missing scene and lost monologue had gone unnoticed and somehow unmissed. He felt in retrospect it had worked better with the cuts we had unintentionally made and that the play had taken on a new quality and unity from the three of us in the second half following the incident. I was truly amazed.

So, I lived to fight another day and remain eternally grateful to my lovely fellow actors for their timely brave rescue and to a director generous with second chances.

***

So, what happens if we forget the words to our song? What if we are suddenly 'stopped' with no idea what we should say or do next in our lives? I hope this little story can serve as a reminder of some of the ways God redeems situations of failure or of crisis for us.

Just as in my story, maybe there are two scripts that collide – the old and the new version of the song. I believe that when David says he has *hidden the word of God in his heart* that he might not sin against Him (Psalm 119:11), he gives a great example to us. If we are stuck or in crisis, the Bible is like a lamp that will light our path (see Psalm 119:105).

Some days when we are reading the Bible and perhaps it doesn't seem particularly relevant or pertinent to our circumstances, I think we are still storing up a script in our mind and soul that we will one day need to draw on. The words of Jesus are an amazing script to learn and study as we repeat and rehearse truth for our lives. When we are stuck His words can infiltrate our words and thoughts, and influence what happens next.

In the Old Testament, in the book of Exodus, Moses has just such a moment of panic. He is sure that he won't know the words to say to lead the people and to speak to Pharaoh on their behalf. He even says, 'Since I speak with faltering lips, why would Pharaoh listen to me?' (Exodus 6:30). But God reassures Moses that Aaron his brother will stand with him in the gap, that He will use them both in this situation.

> [Aaron] will speak to the people for you, and it will be as if he were your mouth and as if you were God to him. (Exodus 4:16)

The two wonderful actors who came to my rescue helped redeem my 'stuckness' and in the same way I really do believe that God sends people just in time to save us and to move us forwards. He can redeem those moments of shame, of forgetting, of failure, and use those around us to 'enter stage left' on time and lift and help us.

Failure, by the way, is something that I'm always keen to talk about, and even celebrate as it is one of the best teachers and motivators in finding our lost song.

HOW DO PORCUPINES MAKE LOVE?

'Blessed are the meek for they will inherit the earth.' Matthew 5:5

As a church, it can of course be said that we attract all sorts. In fact, that is the mandate of the kingdom of God, to be the net that gathers in fish of every kind. Philip was one of those interesting 'fish' that potentially can cause the most upheaval for a pastor and yet, for us as a church family, he was one of our greatest teachers.

Philip came to us as a church nomad, proud of the fact that he never stayed anywhere for long. He was banned from many cafes and bars in our locality for inappropriate behaviour. He suffered with schizophrenia and had what would be diagnosed now as bipolar disorder. Philip wrote me the worst emails I have ever received but equally some of the most kind and grateful. He was looking for family, for community and for a young wife, something that caused us some very delicate and difficult conversations across the church! Philip never read the unspoken nuances of church behaviour. If you were preaching and asked a rhetorical question you would always get an extremely loud answer from Philip. If he had enjoyed your talk, he would shout out 'well done!' in his usual unrestraine and joyful tones. If I was ever feeling a bit shaky at the end of a preach then to hear his 'well done' often meant so much to me. I loved the fact that Philip was spontaneously grateful. I loved the fact he didn't always know the right way to behave in sermons!

Philip was also rather hard of hearing which made prayer meetings very interesting as people are inclined to use more whispery tones in group prayer. I remember one time when we were praying for the Olympic Games, our little group had been allocated Canada and Venezuela as our countries to pray for. Philip prayed loudly and heartily for Canada. *God bless Canada, Lord, and may they do well in the games but get far fewer medals than the United Kingdom.*

So that's Canada sort of covered, now for Venezuela. Mike began to pray earnestly for the country of Venezuela in such hushed tones that to Philip it seemed that prayer had dried up and no one was praying. He decided he would tell me a joke to fill the silent interlude. 'How do porcupines make love, Judy?' came Philip's cry. Earnest prayer for Venezuela continued. 'Carefully!' shouted Philip in answer to the joke's question, and then threw back his head and laughed raucously. And so, we prayed on for Venezuela with shaking shoulders and tears of laughter running down our faces.

Sometimes I would walk into cafes (the ones Philip was still allowed to go to at the time), only to be greeted by him shouting across the room: 'I love you, Judy!' He

once told a whole cafe that I was head of the Queen
Elizabeth Hospital in Birmingham as well as leading
our church. He wrote really steamy play scripts and
read them loudly to slightly fragile old ladies and
young girls at church gatherings, while leaders
hovered, intervening when they could.

The miracle in all of this was that Philip stayed.
He knew he was loved, often got things wrong, often
apologised profusely days later and over the years he
began to change. He loved getting together for food
and was always the first to arrive. He grew in love
and understanding, he grew in his knowledge and
awareness of grace and as a result so did we. He left us
once with a great flourish of angry emails detailing the
many reasons he was leaving the church and so we
sent him a card to say that we missed him and that we
would always see him as a loved part of our family The
next week he was back with us and he never left again.

At the age of 80 Philip decided he wanted to get
baptised. In the build up to his baptism there was a bit
of concern about the testimony time.

With his love for the totally inappropriate and his
ability to misread a situation, what would Philip say
when given the free reign of a microphone and the
opportunity to address the whole gathered church?

'Philip why have you decided to get baptised today?',
I asked, praying silently. The church collectively held
their breath.

'I'm a sinner, saved by grace!' came the reply loud and clear. That was it, nothing more, nothing less. Philip had found grace; he was loved, accepted and forgiven and he knew it. Beautiful.

Two years later Philip died. I was worried about the funeral. Philip was estranged from nearly all his living family, having offended them so many times over the years. When we announced the date of the funeral, I asked the church if we could show our love for Philip now in death as we had done in his life by showing up for him. On the day of the funeral it was pouring with rain, and the service was right in the middle of the working day. With deterrents like this, I asked myself, who would come? What if hardly anyone did?

I busied myself at the front, checking microphones and lectern etc and, as the organ began to play, I turned. The church was packed, rammed with church family, and even some of Philip's own family had decided to come. As I gave the eulogy, I thanked the family for the gift of their brother to us as a church, explaining that he had made us more loving, more fun, more kind, and, despite the pain of some of his earthly struggles, Philip had given us a gift. He had helped us learn to love with tenacity, with clean slates and open hearts. He had been our teacher and we are richer for having known him. Now he was free from all that had limited him in life, his beautiful soul free and unfettered by human struggle.

We left the crematorium an hour later under huge black umbrellas. Philip's sister turned to me and asked, 'How did you manage to love our brother? He was just so difficult to love.'

'I didn't do it alone,' I replied. 'His whole church did and he loved us so well too.'

Philip's brother asked me, 'How do you know that someone like our brother is with God and is forgiven for all those dreadful things? Does God tell you?'

At that moment we looked up to see a beautiful rainbow arching across the rainy sky. 'Maybe that's from Phil telling us this time he's alright,' said Philip's brother.

I explained that, in the Bible, rainbows are a sign that God is faithful. What better way for God to let us know, this time Philip really is alright.

So, what can be learned from the story of Philip? I think one very important lesson is that mental health is an area that the Bible doesn't ignore in the way that maybe the Church sometimes has. We all have good and bad mental health and, just as with our physical health, it fluctuates. Some, like Philip, struggle more extremely and need extra love, grace and understanding.

Elijah, Job and David are all characters in the Bible who show fragility in their mental health. God 's advice and gradual healing for them comes through advising on eating and drinking, resting, belonging – and helping them to lament and express pain. For Job, he hears and sees God in creation and realises He is still in control. For David, there is forgiveness and healing from shame as he pours his heart out with incredible vulnerability and authentic confession. For Elijah, he is caused to rest and eat and rediscover perspective.

Jesus introduced what some might refer to as Christian mindfulness when he taught us to take each day as it comes and live in the moment by being fully present with God and with people. He told us His peace was a gift He would leave with each of us. There is a beautiful Hebrew word 'shalom' that reflects God's deep desire for us to experience wellbeing and His best plan for our lives. His heart for us is that we would be healed by the 'shalom' of His peace through His creation and through the beauty and love of His people.

I believe that those of us who already know we are part of God's family have a key role to play in helping all people to sing, in helping every person know that it takes a choir, a chorus, to build community; it's not a solo performance. It interests me that being part of a choir has been shown to be a hugely healing factor for our mental health and wellbeing. We were made to sing together, to listen to each other.

Surely we can be the context for vulnerability and fragility as we love each other not just as the people we first meet but as the people we see that, with more and more grace, we may be one day.

Life teachers like Philip will rarely seem to us like our teachers when we first meet them, but sometimes the people who are hardest to love are the ones we learn from the most!

'Mental health is defined as a state of well-being in which every individual realizes his or her full potential, can cope with the normal stresses of life, can work productively and fruitfully, and is able to contribute to her or his community.'
(World Health Organization)[2]

SEVEN

Retreat
Runaway

'When we make room for silence, we make room for ourselves. Silence invites the unknown, the untamed, the wild, the shy, the unfathomable, that which rarely has a chance to surface within us.'
Gunilla Norris

'[There is] a time to tear and a time to mend, a time to be silent and a time to speak' Ecclesiastes 3:7

'Be still, and know that I am God... Selah.'
Psalm 46:10-11

Some lovely friends had paid for my first-ever residential spiritual retreat, so I packed up my blue Beetle in Birmingham with a mild sense of fear and trepidation, as well as the excitement of a new experience and adventure.

Would I be able to stay quiet? What if I was overcome by the desire to laugh raucously in the middle of the whispering stillness? As someone who quite often feels irreverent, how would I rein in my propensity for chatter and spontaneous laughter? A lovely friend of mine, who talks even more than me, refers to using 'our inside voices' as, when entering a museum in Berlin, a young guide suggested that she might like to use her 'inside voice' – this still makes us laugh whenever we think about it.

As I arrived and walked around the old and extremely cold building, I felt immediately awkward and out of place. This was definitely a place for the inside voice – there would be silence at mealtimes, a spiritual guide and lots of chances to reflect in stillness and solitude, none of which I must confess come particularly naturally to me. I was nevertheless ready for the adventure and excited about a new community for my week-long stay.

An unsmiling welcomer told me that there was no heating as the boiler needed mending, and then gave me my list of chores. I couldn't help but think of the equally long list of chores I had left at home but realised this was all part of this new community experience. One of my chores would be to feed the chickens and this created a new source of panic based on my bird phobia and general suspicion of their motives and behaviour.

I was shown to my dormitory where someone was lying in bed shivering and coughing with a fever.

Apologetically I left my bag on the opposite bed and tried not to rush out of there too quickly. I felt like I had somehow stumbled into a scene from an early nineteenth century Charles Dickens novel where the protagonist was a church leader going through a breakup who had unknowingly been sent to a punitive institution!

I walked into the large library in search of my designated spiritual director, only to be told that my one wasn't going to be available for the week! Stumbling around up and down the corridors my despair increased. Lunch was to be the first gathering where I would meet my new community. As a natural extrovert (with introvert leanings) I felt things would surely start to pick up.

Rachmaninoff pealed forth from the dining room as I approached. We would eat our soup and bread, unsmiling and in silence as we listened to the music's discordant lament. I spiralled further into melancholy.

Later that afternoon, I sat shivering in a large leather chair wondering who or what I had offended to deserve this. I dug deep and tried to be still and 'enter in' as we were being advised to do but after just an hour, I was bored, cold, tearful and couldn't wait for dinner when we could finally speak. I would finally meet my fellow inmates and we could all have a good old laugh about how awful it all was (a much-valued coping mechanism of mine).

However, at dinner, the community I had joined turned in on itself. They seemed to be journeying together and all knew each other – leaving me an outsider. So, having gone for a walk after dinner and having completed my chores for the day (avoiding chickens as much as possible), I thought I would just go to bed. Sometimes things look much better after a good night's sleep!

My twelve-person dormitory (with the poor girl with flu) didn't really lend itself to anything close to a good night's sleep. I had come away to heal, to be still, to regroup, to press 'CTRL-ALT-DELETE' on a painful chapter in my life and to gain perspective. Instead, I felt I had probably gained a nasty flu bug, a hatred for Rachmaninoff and a vow never to be silent again, so in the dark, I put my clothes back on, wrote a letter of apology to the hosts and crept down the creaking Dickensian staircase out into the night.

A retreat runaway. A newly appointed church leader in flight from a Christian retreat. Not a good look!

An embarrassing postscript to the episode was that in my hurry I left a stiletto boot in the dormitory and was too embarrassed to go back. My brother-in-law popped in on his way past some days later to ask about the whereabouts of an abandoned high-heeled boot!

So, what can be learned from this cautionary tale of the retreat runaway?

Although I totally understand that the timing and circumstances of my stay didn't go well, there was still a deeper lesson. We all need to find what works for us. Silence and stillness are a vital part of spiritual formation and renewal, but they will look so different for each one of us. I know other people who have gone to the very same place and have had a really healing time.

I have since been on some wonderful sensory retreats which helped me to reflect and be still, with focus on visual natural beauty, with food and tasting and sensory engagement. I had been in the wrong place for me at the wrong time but just days later I was in a cottage in Norfolk reflecting and journaling to my heart's content with beach walks nearby and a big open fire on my return.

We all need to find our own stillness, our own silences, our own ways of renewing the soul. Jesus walked up mountains, sat in solitude away from the clamouring crowds and showed us that we need to do the same. I would also dare to say that silence and stillness can be fun. We can enjoy God, His humour and His love – it doesn't have to be sombre and in a minor key!

I sometimes wonder if a bird's song is rehearsed in silence and then out of this comes the joy and splendour of a morning dawn chorus. I'm guessing though there is no such rehearsal, just a silent readiness to sing again.

If we are to have song for life there will be times, like the birds, for stillness and for silence before we break into our song.

Selah is a musical term used in some of the psalms to increase their power. It is used 72 times in the Psalms. It signifies a time to pause, to stop. If we are to find our song, we may need to find the pauses, the silences, that will punctuate and enhance it.

In the Bible, Ecclesiastes chapter 3 talks about there being a time and season for everything under heaven. It is such a beautiful reminder that there are times when silence and stillness are as vital an action as hard work is at others. Our song will include it all and will benefit from our pauses and our stillness. French philosopher, Blaise Pascal, is known to have said, 'All humanity's problems stem from man's inability to sit quietly in a room alone.' In the silence we can listen, reflect and renew our thinking.

There is a time for us all to be still, to be silent. There is also a time to stay and a time to run away.

EIGHT

WELL DONE FOR BEING HERE

'Jesus reveals a God who does not demand but who gives; who does not oppress but who raises up; who does not wound but heals.'
Brennan Manning

'Fear not, for I have redeemed you; I have called you by name, you are mine. When you pass through the waters, I will be with you; and through the rivers, they shall not overwhelm you'
Isaiah 43:1-2, ESV

Brian was an elderly member of our church. He was somehow on the welcome team by his own appointment. He was not in the best of health mentally or physically. He found church services noisy and difficult to deal with, often preferring to sit outside. No one had asked him to join the welcome team and his self-selection had gone unchallenged but certainly not unnoticed. He wore his own lanyard saying 'I'm an epileptic' rather than the uniform bright yellow 'Hello' lanyard worn by everyone else on the team. He looked like a rather forlorn Father Christmas who found himself in the middle of summer, not sure of his role.

For us, as leaders, he presented a dilemma, Brian didn't really fit the image of a happening and relevant multi-site church in the city, welcoming people in with bright shiny young smiles. He was old, unkempt and sometimes, if I'm honest, rather grumpy! We decided, if what mattered to him was to make people welcome, then that was the role he should play.

Lindsay is part of my prayer group and has been a friend of mine for many years. One day she found her husband, Trevor, dead on the bathroom floor. There was no real warning, no chance to save him, to pray for his rescue. He was gone aged just 51. The shock, the incredible suddenness of his loss, meant the pain was deeply raw, almost *too* raw, for people, even her loving church family, to know what to say. Going to church became an enormous challenge for her with the biggest hurdle of all being getting past the smiling welcome team. When people sincerely asked her how she was doing, she was scared she might tell them, maybe at the top of her voice that she was in deep dark pain, bewildered, desperate. How do you answer that famous British question 'How are you today?' with honesty, especially to loving well-wishers who just want everything to be alright?

One Sunday not long after Trevor's death, Lindsay made her brave but faltering way through our church car park. She stopped to pray. *Please Lord just get me through the welcome line, help me pass through invisibly immune to their smiling questions and well-meant inquiry.*

Lindsay walked through the entrance to the church and was greeted by Brian who was, on this day, to be the beautiful messenger of Jesus, the answer to the prayer uttered just minutes before, a herald of heaven wearing a lanyard saying, 'I'm an epileptic'.

'Well done for being here today.' And that was it, that was all Brian said. He had no idea about what had happened in Lindsay's life; he didn't know the pain she carried, he just sensed the voice of Jesus saying *well done for being here* and he said it.

For me, this is church at its messy, most precarious best. When someone's song is muted, when we have lost the ability to stand, even to sing, God, I believe, sends us His messengers, His angels in human form, to help us, to cheer us on. Lindsay tells me that was truly the best thing anyone could have said to her that day in her grief, yet Brian has no idea how his 'song' lifted Lindsay. He has no idea that his calling, his purpose was to be in the right place at the right time, ready to listen, to be used by God.

Sometimes that's what we need most: someone to say *well done for being here*, for showing up to life, to work, to the party. Well done for getting dressed rather than staying in bed, well done for holding on to faith when what has happened is such a pain-filled mystery.

It can seem as if our song – our life – has stopped, when grief comes along and takes our breath away, making us forget our words, making us stumble. The light goes out and we can't see. But God has promised to help us. He has said He is close to the broken-hearted, that He will send help. Sometimes we will be the one in need of that help, stumbling around in the car park, afraid to show up. Sometimes we can be the unknowing, unassuming messenger of comfort. The one whose song touched the life of another in the most profound way. We can be chosen, not by man, but by God himself to sing. A bird in tune with its creator somehow just knows what to sing and so too can we.

There is a great deal of teaching in the Bible about the least and the last – those who perhaps have been neglected or ostracised by community – finding a place, a purpose and a home.

David is a small shepherd boy who steps in to slay Goliath (the giant warrior of the day). He is victorious because he comes in the name of the living God. He aligns the song of his life to God, and he is used by God in an incredible way. Unlikely people are the Bible's speciality, and Brian was the unlikely choice to bring God's loving kindness to Lindsay that day. We too can be the unlikely choice, even this very day, if we step up like Brian and say *I'm available, take my song and use it for someone else.*

IS THAT HELICOPTER FOR ME?

> 'The decision to grow always involves a choice between risk and comfort. This means that to be a follower of Jesus you must renounce comfort as the ultimate value of your life.' John Ortberg

I was on a tour with a theatre company and Philip and Janet Yancey, sharing theatrical illustrations of Philip's brilliant book *What Good is God?* We were touring Australia and New Zealand and we had a few days off to enjoy the wonders of Queenstown on New Zealand's beautiful South Island. Queenstown has been referred to as the adventure capital of the world!

We (the three actors in the company) had been given three days off and were staying in a beautiful lake and mountainside retreat centre. We decided that each of us would choose one activity that we really wanted to do, and the others would do their best to join in. I chose a visit to hot natural pools and we all had a wonderful day of rest and relaxation (admittedly not quite the adrenalin-inducing activities associated with this adventure capital, but it was blissful!).

The next choice, from Michael (our youngest and most daring member), was the inevitable Queenstown bungee jump. Our 'joining in' for this was to cheer loudly, to hold things, to film things and to watch endless camera reruns when we returned to our retreat centre.

The third and final day was David's choice and was called the Shotover Jet. 'Churning rapids and towering cliffs' declared the advertisement, 'a high-speed jet will have you spinning and fishtailing across the water'.

The offer included round-trip transport in the form of a coach journey to the edge of the river canyon. The three of us boarded the coach ready to get to our destination riding those churning rapids. We settled in and I sat by the window ready to admire the mountainous view. At this point our driver told us in Kiwi-style humour that he had only had a 'couple of cold ones' (beers) and that he didn't have too many tingles down his right arm now and so should be fine to drive us through the black ice on this cliff-edge trip.

The more anxious we appeared, the more he seemed to speed up, rather like the fairground ride where they shout, 'The louder you scream the faster we will go!' Only this wasn't a fairground ride, this was about seventy people, many of them children, being driven way too fast on black ice on the edge of a cliff.

I was terrified and really angry, so much so that at one point our daredevil driver shouted, 'If I can just make that lady at the back smile it will have been a good ride!' I am not remotely ashamed to say that lady was me... fuming!

Very sweetly, Michael leaned over and let me put one of his earphones in to listen to some worship music with him. Incredibly he was listening to Matt Redman's song *You Never Let Go.*

Miraculously, we did arrive safely and descended from the coach, adrenalin pumping and, in my case, legs shaking. I was still angry and declared to both David and Michael that I wouldn't be joining them on the speed boat ride as I couldn't trust the driver or the company that would employ someone so irresponsible!

At that moment a helicopter appeared in the sky. In my heightened dramatic (some might add diva) state, I asked the guys if they could see if the helicopter was indeed there to pick me up and take me back to our mountainside retreat. Honestly, I was so upset that I was completely serious!

It's fair to say that the helicopter did not take me back, and the question 'Is that helicopter for me?' has often made it into the tour quotation highlights.

Thankfully, David quietly went to speak to our coach driver, who reassured him that he had nothing to do with things from here and would not be the person driving us on the water. The man driving us was someone who had grown up on the canyon and who knew every single twist and turn of its rocks and churning rapids.

This next ride was the one that was billed for fear and adrenalin but felt so amazing compared to our coach trip. Here the driver was a wonderfully reassuring presence with a smiling, confident humility who wanted us to enjoy the ride safely.

It really does all depend on who is in the driving seat!

***

It has been said that 'Faith' is spelt 'RISK'. I often wonder in what areas of my life am I avoiding living out radical faith in favour of a comfortable mediocrity? Am I living too carefully and pragmatically? Although I believe that common sense still plays a key role in guidance and living out our faith, I'm longing for more moments when, like Peter, I jump out of the boat into the depths of the lake.

Author Corrie ten Boom loved the words from Psalm 32 and her father frequently read them from the family Bible:

> You are my hiding-place; you will protect me from trouble and surround me with songs of deliverance. (Psalm 32:7)

She loved the psalm not because she was in any way anesthetised from trouble, but because they were surrounded by presence and power in the midst of trouble. Corrie and her family lived out audacious faith in choosing to hide Jews in the war, putting their own lives at risk. Her later teaching always reflected her discovery, in the hardest of times, that the safest place was in the very centre of God's will. Yet for Corrie that often took her to places of great risk and danger.

When the writer of the Hebrews lists his faith heroes they are certainly not of the 'stay at home, play it safe' kind. He affirms how 'faith is confidence in what we hope for and assurance about what we do not see' (Hebrews 11:1).

Compare with me for a moment the two drivers in this chapter's story. The first was a reckless, untrustworthy performer looking to promote himself and give everyone a scare. The second was someone who had grown up in the canyon and who wanted us to adventure in safety and celebrate all that he had learned. Faith is risky but in the long run it's all about who we are putting our faith and trust in.

In the Old Testament, Shadrach, Meshach and Abednego walk into the fire only to find that a fourth figure becomes visible with them in the furnace. 'I see four men walking around in the fire, unbound and unharmed, and the fourth looks like a son of the gods' (Daniel 3:25). As we step out in faith, so He steps in with us! There are amazing accounts globally from persecuted Christians testifying to an incredible presence with them, sustaining them.

In theatre practice there is a trust exercise that is often used in team building to grow trust between actors. Once you are in pairs, one of you is blindfolded and told to fall backwards into the partner's arms.

You are reassured that you will hear your partner's voice guiding and reassuring you. They will tell you when to fall when they are ready. All is well until you hear their voice move from behind you to in front of you yet still telling you they are ready for you to fall backwards. What happens next depends on how much the person who is blindfolded trusts their catcher. The ultimate decision for the blindfolded one is about the partner's character not their own. Many fall backwards and find that their partner has selected a catcher to secretly step in behind while they stand in front. Others refuse to budge or stumble forward towards the voice refusing to trust in what can't be fully seen.

This simple drama game speaks profoundly to me about what faith looks like, reflecting the relationship between faith and fear. Fear was so dominant for me on the coach trip because I didn't trust the driver at all, but if we know a driver is for us and for our good then we can trust that he will catch us, he knows us and he knows the way he takes us too!

Our leaps, steps or falls of faith will only increase as we get to know the one who is in control. God is good and completely trustworthy. He knows every twist and turn of the canyon and has even grown up there in the form of His Son Jesus experiencing so many of the trials that we face. Jesus is the one who silently stepped in to catch us. God may send a helicopter on occasions where we see his dramatic intervention but many more times, He lets us ride it out with Him, trusting that He is with us and for us.

Let's not settle for safe, mediocre faith where comfort is what we truly value; let's hold on tight in an adventure knowing a loving God is driving this thing called 'life'.

He will not let your foot slip – he who watches over you will not slumber (Psalm 121:3)

AM I IN THE RIGHT PLACE?

'In their hearts humans plan their course, but the LORD establishes their steps.' Proverbs 16:9

'It is all decided by chance [*qarah*], by being in the right place at the right time.' Ecclesiastes 9:11, NLT

It was a Monday evening like any other. He was early, nervous and hovering near the door. We were hosting an evening for the wider leadership team at church (for clarity, these are not people with a slightly wider girth than others, it is what we call the team that extends widely over all our volunteers' teams!). I didn't recognise him and began to panic slightly. How was it that someone was in a leadership position in our church and I didn't remember ever setting eyes on him? I approached tentatively, asking him if he had received all the information for the evening session and if he wanted to get his badge from the welcome table, hoping he might then help me remember his name.

He asked me how long I had been coming to the group and I said I thought that it was over four years.

He looked totally baffled. 'Really?' he declared with incredulity, 'That's full on!'

I agreed yes, it's a lot of work but it really pays off and it's a great way of getting to know everyone well.

'Yes,' he agreed, looking increasingly uncertain and suspicious.

He turned very shy suddenly and started looking down at the literature I had foisted on him ready for the evening. 'I'm not sure I'm in the right place,' he said in an almost inaudible voice, still looking down. I was about to launch into a reassuring speech about how none of us really felt like we fitted a leadership role and how we had that sense of imposter syndrome associated with taking on responsibility, when something slowly started to dawn on me. A few weeks earlier, we had signed off on a request for a group to use an upstairs room in the church building every Monday evening. It was a closed group for male sex addicts!

To my acute embarrassment I began to replay the last five minutes especially the bit where I had told him I had been attending for over four years. No wonder he had looked so horrified!

'There is another group meeting tonight,' I said tentatively, '*It's just for men, I think.*'

'Oh yeah, that's the one I think,' he replied, and with that he made his escape clutching the literature I had handed him in his rush to get away!

Some years later, on a Monday night, we were hosting a different event about fostering and adopting with the brilliant charity Home for Good, and I was welcoming on the door again. A young man walked in and I had that slight feeling of *déjà vu*.

'I'm not quite sure where I should go,' he said, smiling. Not recognising him as a member of our church and unaware that our brilliant children's worker had opened the event up to other churches, I resolved not to repeat my mistake of all those years ago.

'Don't worry,' I said in a conspiratorial whisper, 'I think you need to just go straight upstairs and into the room to your left.'

He thanked me and quickly made his way upstairs. How sad, I thought to myself, that someone so lovely is caught up in addiction.

Fast forward five minutes and I glance across the room and see the very same man looking flustered and sitting down with his fostering pack and workbook for the event. This time I had sent a pastoral leader from another city church unknowingly into a sex addict support group where he had spent five minutes discovering who knows what!

I'm sure, by now, you are wondering how on earth I'm allowed to be a pastor and would be even more concerned to know that I'm safeguarding lead and in charge of people-care across our church. I frequently wonder the same thing.

Part of the process of us finding our song and fulfilling our unique purpose comes from being in the right place at the right time. But at certain times in our lives I'm sure we feel much more like the two guys in this cautionary tale: lost, confused and in the wrong place and following the wrong, albeit well-meaning, leads!

Qarah is the Hebrew word for being in the right place at the right time. We see the word in Ecclesiastes 9:11. However, it doesn't simply mean chance; it literally means 'by God's appointment'. There are so many times in our lives when we are somewhere, not by chance, but by God's appointment, whether we realise it or not.

In the Bible, Ruth has her *qarah* moment when she is working away in the field of the man Boaz. She is widowed and living with deep loss and pain, yet Ruth has been faithful, following her mother-in-law, Naomi, with so much loyalty and compassion, declaring, 'Don't urge me to leave you or turn back from you. Where you go I will go' (Ruth 1:16). She is pledging such generous allegiance to Naomi and is trusting in God that, if she is obedient, she will end up in the right place.

It is while working hard and trusting in God that her kindness and demeanour attracts the attention of Boaz who will become not only the one she marries, but also the one who saves and redeems her whole family.

The story of Ruth speaks to me on many levels, and has done so at key points in my Christian life. Once, when I cried out to God when things had taken a very sudden dramatic turn in my life, the verse that I felt God highlighting for me was Psalm 37:3: 'Trust in the LORD and do good... in the land.' If I'm honest, it wasn't the verse I wanted. I wanted a different verse, one about everything working out and coming good! Trust sounds hard, and it often is, but equally, I do believe it can lead us to those moments of *qarah*, those times when we keep on keeping on, looking outwards and upwards rather than staring at our own feet!

Ruth is a beautiful example of someone who could have stayed home, overtaken and consumed by pain. Yet hers is a wonderful story of someone who finds her song again through courage and obedience. She follows the God she is only just beginning to get to know to a land she doesn't know at all and finds this new God so faithful that even her mother-in-law (who once said her name would always be *mara* meaning 'empty') becomes blessed.

I believe God has divine appointments for every one of us: those dates and places in our diaries, those meetings at the gym, those chats waiting for the train that seem so random but are nevertheless part of God's divine plan.

We can be the answer to someone's prayer, the rescuer who steps in with a smile, a message of hope, or a text of encouragement.

If today there is a sense that you are in the wrong place, that your song is confused or on mute, that you are somehow stuck, I hope that you are encouraged to keep walking, to keep trusting, to keep looking to 'do good in the land' and to pray and believe for those moments of *qarah* that will surely come, where you suddenly say, 'This is where I'm meant to be!'

Losing
your voice

'Hope is the thing with feathers
That perches in the soul,
And sings the tune without the words,
And never stops at all.'
Emily Dickinson

'He who overcomes, I will make him a pillar in the temple of My God' Revelation 3:12, NKJV

I'd always been slightly judgmental about people losing their voices completely. I guess I felt they were hamming it up, enjoying it even. I would openly suggest to actors and singers that perhaps they hadn't been using their voices properly when they found themselves vocally challenged like that. Well sure enough, pride comes before a fall and there it was, I woke up one day to find that I could barely speak. *Serves you right* I hear you cry! I now know it really is a thing and indeed how much of a thing it really is.

I was due to speak at an event for women that very night and as the day wore on, I was pretty sure I couldn't utter a word, let alone speak for the required forty minutes. By lunchtime I had emailed the organiser to let her know my predicament, secretly hoping that they would begin to at least consider a Plan B, if not put it into motion.

The cheery reply pinged back, reassuring me of the teams' fervent prayers and of their great anticipation of all the Lord would share through my words that evening. *What words exactly?* I thought, as I made incoherent rasping sounds at work and even put myself on vocal rest, a phrase I had previously scorned.

A few hours later and I arrived at the venue tentatively walking into the vestibule to find the team hard at prayer. I joined in with a slightly sinking heart. They were excited about all they expected God to do thorough the word and ministry. I wanted to interrupt and throatily ask if they had got the message that I couldn't speak, wondering just what it was they were excited to hear from a speaker on mute.

A truly lovely lady took me to a side chapel of the church where I hoped she might give me a hot water or a throat sweet but instead I was immediately anointed with oil on my forehead and prayed for once again. Why don't Christians get it, I was arguing to myself, who is not able to understand that my voice has gone and why aren't they looking at other last-minute options instead of me? Each time I tried to speak to a member of the team I was encouraged not to, which in retrospect was probably a very good thing!

The evening began with some sung worship and the crowds were gathering – around a hundred women – full of buzz and anticipation. I couldn't remember feeling this nervous for years. I tested my voice on one of the songs, only to hear the weird rasping sound joining the cacophony of excited singing! I looked up towards the altar of the church and there inscribed across the stone archway above were these words, *To him who overcomes I will make him a pillar in the temple of my God*. I prayed that this would be true for me somehow, there and then, that I might be one of those overcoming pillars holding up the truth of the word of God.

I walked up to speak on the subject 'Does my faith look big in this?'. My faith did not look or feel that big in that moment. The lady leading the night introduced me, prayed and that was it, I started to speak and yes, that's exactly what I mean, I literally started to speak, my voice gaining power and clarity as I continued. I went on to speak clearly and normally into my radio mic for around forty minutes, culminating in a monologue of Mary at the tomb who in her last line declares that while she has breath in her lungs she cannot help but speak of all she has seen and heard of the story of Jesus Christ! On boldly declaring that line my voice was gone once again!

I had experienced a miracle; of that I have no doubt. I had indeed been used as a pillar in the temple, an overcomer even!

These wise women had shown so much resilience and faith and had believed God would speak through and even in spite of me! It was a wonderful reminder that it is God who decides how and when He will speak, and He is so much bigger than us and our faltering faith. It always humbles me when speaking, that sometimes when I feel I have preached well with passion and gusto He doesn't appear to be so evident in the response, while at other times, when I feel fragile and that I have spoken as well as I think I should have, He does amazing things. The Bible says in John 3:8: 'The wind blows wherever it pleases. You hear its sound, but you cannot tell where it comes from or where it is going. So it is with everyone born of the Spirit'.

The miraculous is full of mystery and, for me, mystery and miracle are often allies, often strange bedfellows at work in the same stories. I totally know I have experienced miracles in health, in provision, in overcoming adversity, but I also, like nearly all of us, live with the complete mystery of seemingly unanswered prayer.

There are surely times in all of our lives when we feel our voice is on mute. As if the bird has not only forgotten the words but has lost the heart or capacity to sing. Sudden grief and loss, disappointment, a deadly diagnosis… and our voice and our words run out. How will we become those who rediscover our song, those *overcoming pillars in the temple of God*?

In the Bible, in the book of Job, we see a man who has his song seemingly snatched away from him. He is stripped of so much of his life. He loses his livestock, his servants, his children and he is covered with painful sores. Even his wife turns against him and his friends do more harm than good with their attempts to make sense of it all. They suggest a type of 'try harder, pray longer spirituality' not uncommon in our own faltering attempts to make sense of mystery and undeserved pain. But out of the darkness and the shadows, God finally speaks, and when He does, it is spectacular. In some of the most beautiful words in the Bible, coming after some of the most agonising words of questioning, God speaks of His absolute sovereignty.

In chapters 38 to 41, God speaks to Job of all the wonder and majesty of creation. He reminds Job that He has done all the creating, the forming of the world. He asks him if he was there when He laid the foundations of the earth for example, or if he, Job, has ever journeyed to the very source of the sea? This might seem a bit unfair on Job in all the agony of his underserved tragedy, but what I believe God is so powerfully saying is, 'I am magnified in the mystery and I am way bigger than your sight, experience or understanding of what is really going on!' He is totally beyond our understanding, but He is good, and He is God over it all.

C.S. Lewis once said of Aslan, the lion depicting God in the Chronicles of Narnia: *No He is not safe, but He is good* (my paraphrase). He will never be small enough for us to understand but we don't need Him to be, we need Him to be bigger! God paints a beautiful picture of His creative and sustaining role in the whole of the universe and reassures Job that there are things he cannot yet see or understand in full. Job's response is so full of gratitude and revelation as he declares in 42:3,5: 'Surely I spoke of things I did not understand, things too wonderful for me to know... My ears had heard of you but now my eyes have seen you.' The irony once again is that, in the greatest of trials, he has somehow seen and experienced God's true character and found that it is good.

Of course, to temporarily lose my voice doesn't come close to loss or tragedy but the story does highlight for me the continuing mystery of prayer in my life. Faith is both fragile and mighty at the same time, and overcoming often happens when those around us refuse to give up when we are barely hanging on. Prayer absolutely works, absolutely changes us and our situations and perspective, yet remains mysterious in the how and the why of its miracles. May our hope keep on singing the tune even when we don't have all the words!

Now we see things imperfectly, like puzzling reflections in a mirror, but then we will see everything with perfect clarity. All that I now know is partial and incomplete, but then I will know everything completely, just as God now knows me completely. (1 Corinthians 13:12, NLT)

TWELVE

THE TRAUMA OF THE TABLE

'The voice of sin is loud, but the voice of forgiveness is louder.' D.L. Moody

'To be a Christian means to forgive the inexcusable because God has forgiven the inexcusable in you.' C.S. Lewis

'He does not punish us for all our sins; he does not deal harshly with us, as we deserve. For his unfailing love toward those who fear him is as great as the height of the heavens above the earth. He has removed our sins as far from us as the east is from the west.' Psalm 103:10–12, NLT

Adrian and Bridget Plass have become wonderful friends of mine over the years, and we have toured and collaborated on some interesting projects, supporting Adrian's brilliant writing with live theatre and the occasional workshop.

It was one such occasion when Adrian and I were co-facilitating a workshop exploring the tricky subject of forgiveness. We opened the floor for people to share their own real-life experiences of forgiveness and what it costs. Adrian is a uniquely gifted writer and pastoral man who deals with people in a beautifully reassuring and valuing way. In his wonderful gentle manner, he asked who felt able to share and a lovely Scottish lady began to speak, shakily yet courageously, of her incredible journey of painful forgiveness. Her husband had been arrested for viewing pornographic images and allegedly abusing children. He was a dad and loving husband, yet suddenly she had been thrown into this tumult of pain when all was discovered, and he was taken away and imprisoned. She had somehow – through much prayer, wrestling and ministry – arrived at a place of forgiveness and reconciliation. She had realised that to hold on to toxic bitterness was to rob her family of even more than they had already lost, and she movingly spoke of setting them all free by forgiving her husband.

It was the first time this lovely woman had been able to share this publicly and there was an almost audible gasp as we all dried our eyes and applauded both her grace in arriving at this place of forgiveness and her courage to share such a raw ongoing life experience.

Bearing in mind it would be incredibly hard to follow this with another story with equal levels of shock and trauma, before long, another much more confident voice began to share. This lady assured us that there were some things like this, that in time you could forgive but that, every now and then, something happened that she didn't really see you could or even should forgive. We all steeled ourselves for what must surely follow, something so horrendous that the grace and mercy experienced and demonstrated by the previous lady could not even reach. Our new contributor told of a church bazaar where she had managed to secure a large trestle table ideal for the children's toys and bric-a-brac she was about to display in fundraising for a good cause. All was prepared and ready when she was called away and distracted by a request for her assistance. Imagine her horror and dismay when she returned to find the table that she had so faithfully prepared had been taken away to be used somewhere else and the perpetrator of this heinous crime was nowhere to be seen. Soon it was revealed who was responsible for this seemingly unforgivable act of sabotage. There was no apology nor remorse. She had therefore concluded that here was something that she was not inclined or maybe even called to let go of. What did people think?

Could we join her in concluding that there were some things that are just plain wrong and beyond our capacity and inclination to forgive?

Because Adrian is Adrian, he masterfully honoured this lady's heartfelt disclosure with as much grace and dignity as the previous one. There was no belittling, no correction, just acceptance and thanks for the sincerity of her contribution.

A couple of hours later, driving away from this slightly surreal episode, I began to unpack what I had just been witness to. My first emotion (as is quite often the case) was a need to laugh out loud at the sheer incongruity of it all. I wanted to pull over, call Adrian and laugh hysterically at the madness and occasional absurdity of the Christian life.

I then felt slightly angrier at the judgmental display that had followed so clumsily after such a beautiful demonstration of what real grace can undo.

It was then that God began to challenge me. Am I any different?

Why is it that I can dig deep and find grace and forgiveness for the really big things of life and fester and quarrel with Him on some of the much smaller things?

Grace is indiscriminate. The grace and forgiveness of Jesus covered both the legalism of the Pharisee and the penitence of a thief on the cross. The lady with the husband's betrayal and the lady with the table thief each had the choice, and each had their own inner battle to resolve things both with the perpetrator and with God!

The heart of the Christian faith is forgiveness. It is unique in our DNA.

In every other world faith, it seems, there is an onus on us, the follower, to do better, to try harder. The Christian follows Jesus Christ whose dying words were *it is finished*. Supposedly, Buddha's last words were *strive without ceasing*. So many philosophies and faiths today seem to present us with the ideology of self-salvation.

Yet at heart, isn't it true that most of us know that *try harder* doesn't seem to work? We know the disappointment of failed resolutions, of the mantra of *must do better*. Somehow, deep down, I wonder if we ache for the fresh start and freedom Jesus uniquely offers us. As we read in 1 Peter 1:3: 'Praise be to the God and Father of our Lord Jesus Christ! In his great mercy he has given us new birth into a living hope through the resurrection of Jesus Christ from the dead.'

***

Jesus tells the story of the unmerciful servant who is let off an incredible debt by his master and yet then quibbles with a far more miniscule debt owed to him by a fellow servant (see Matthew 18:21–35). Jesus, in telling this story, touches something within us that I believe we recognise. He offers us complete, total forgiveness for every single way we have ever done wrong or neglected to do good. He covers all of it with that outrageous claim on the cross: *it is finished*.

I'm always reassured by the fact that the only person we absolutely know is in heaven with Jesus was a thief who in his last breath discovered forgiveness. He was told 'today you will be with me in paradise' (Luke 23:43).

As I shared in my first book, I have learned how important it is as a pastor to acknowledge that some things are simply not right. They offend us and offend God. The act of forgiveness does not require us to say that rape, abuse, neglect or oppression are right, far from it! I think the deeper lesson is to say much like our wonderful lady in the story, *this has taken enough from me and I refuse to let it take any more in bitterness.*

This is a process, a posture. Rarely, if ever, is it a one-off transaction but rather an ongoing work of beautiful, transforming grace.

Paul, who wrote almost half of the New Testament, was a murderer, a terrorist, who had killed multiple times. His confession was this:

But God had mercy on me so that Christ Jesus could use me as a prime example of his great patience with even the worst sinners. Then others will realize that they, too, can believe in him and receive eternal life. (1 Timothy 1:16, NLT)

I'll close this chapter with the words from the prayer that Jesus Himself taught us to say: 'forgive us our sins, as we forgive those who sin against us' (Luke 11:4, NLT). Whether it's a disappearing table or a deep, complex family trauma, our need to both give and receive grace perhaps remains the same.

A NEW SOUNDTRACK

'Come to me. Get away with me...
I'll show you how to take a real rest.'
Matthew 11:28–30, *The Message*

If the year 2020 was a film, it has been said that the soundtrack would be birdsong. As I write, we are living in lockdown ordered by the UK Government to halt the spread of Covid-19. The world has changed in a matter of days. It is a very strange feeling knowing we are living through such a key time of struggle that is globally shared. There is a sense of being part of an incredibly significant time in history, knowing that we will never be quite the same again. What began supposedly with a bat in China has evolved into a disease that has literally put the whole world on pause.

Schools, shops, bars, restaurants, theatres, cinemas, cafes are all closed, and we are staying home to shield the most vulnerable from infection. We are isolating and socially distancing across the world. Yet hereby lies the irony; in this strange and enforced time of stillness we are learning to lead a different life.

Our old song of individualism and self-indulgence has been silenced and we are called to sing a new song, with some melodies borrowed from the past.

This week my neighbours and I have had a joint tea over the fence, we have created a new WhatsApp group for our road to share laughter and loss in equal measure. Families are around the table again, singing together, dancing together, holding each other a little bit closer. We are realising the fragility of life that certain generations alive today have never known before. The Italians have been singing to each other in isolation across from their balconies, picking up any instruments they can find. Some police in Majorca drove thought the streets with guitars and sang to all those in captivity in their homes, to encourage them to stay safe and stay home. They are singing a new song, the song of unity in separation, of reaching out to touch hearts while physical touch is denied.

In some adjoining flats in London, two people who had never met started playing piano duets with each other through the wall. After having done this at 2pm every day for some weeks, the young pianist on one side finally goes to meet his neighbour. He discovers the neighbour is a 78 year old polish man, called Emil, who is in temporary accommodation and who has recently lost his wife to Covid-19. The piano is one of the only things he owns, and he plays it every day at the same time in memory of his wife who loved to hear him play. This daily duetting has shown him he is not alone and has helped him with the raw pain of his grief and loneliness. How beautiful to hear how each of these men have found their song is so enriched by joining with another.

A world that was becoming a place of individualism has discovered that we need each other more than we ever have. We need each other's song to join with our own, to lift us up, to connect us in our struggle. Now is not the time for the soloists; it is time for the choir to sing!

I had a moment of feeling deeply alone and lost during this first lockdown. I cried out to God in silent prayer as I sat outside in my garden. Suddenly a voice called out, 'It's tricky on your own Judith.' Was it the very voice of God, I hear you ask! Well, yes and no. In human terms it was the voice of my lovely neighbour Seb who was swinging on his hammock. Seb is a beautiful child inside and out. He is autistic and often his sentences and phrases are those he repeats from books, adverts and TV programmes but this was totally unique. This was a sentence his parents had never heard him say. Seb is an only child and his parents, Zoe and Del, are wonderful and have become such valued friends in lockdown. Apart from a couple of other friends from childhood they are the only people who call me Judith. Having little Seb call out in recognition of a prayer he wouldn't have known I'd said, calling me by my childhood name, was God's way of letting me know I was not alone. He saw me and spoke using the voice of a child to reassure me of His understanding of how I felt.

As the world has been stilled, as we have stopped flying and driving, the world seems to be a cleaner, quieter place. Somebody shared on Facebook:

It feels like we have all been sent to our rooms to think about what we have done with our world.

Of course, for those on the frontline life is busier and more pressured than ever before, but they too are currently stripped of social lives, of enjoying life outside of their homes.

Sitting here in my garden in lockdown, it is a time for a deeper reflection. As church leader Pete Greig recently reminded people on social media: *This is a call, not to diminished life, but to a deeper one.*

In an earlier chapter I wrote about being a 'retreat runaway', not realising that a few months later we would be on an enforced global retreat. Last night, I went for a walk in the park at sunset and was so impacted by the stillness, the clean air and the beauty. We are currently only allowed out of our homes for one time of exercise a day and it is incredible how we are learning to once again 'stop and stare', as the poem goes:

What is this life if, full of care,
We have no time to stand and stare.
No time to see, in broad daylight,
Streams full of stars, like skies at night.
No time to turn at Beauty's glance,
And watch her feet, and how they dance.
(William Henry Davies[3])

Perhaps a song of deeper love is beginning, deeper love for life, for one another and for God. Could it be that this nation which has been labelled 'post-Christian', is turning on its heels, running back into the arms of a prodigal Father who has waited every day for our return?

In this time, as in all times, Jesus is the greatest guide. He told us that we should live each day, a day at a time, and not to worry as we are in His care (see Matthew 6:25–34).

In *The Message* version of the Bible, Jesus' words are paraphrased beautifully:

Get away with me and you'll recover your life. I'll show you how to take a real rest. Walk with me and work with me – watch how I do it. Learn the unforced rhythms of grace. (Matthew 11:28–30)

I really do believe life from here on in will never be the same again, that we have reached a seminal moment in history that will make us search for a deeper life moving forward. I hope and pray that those of us who live through this pandemic live more gratefully and sing again, not as a group of soloists, but as one.

***

I write this now much later in the year 2020 and we have lost so many lives as a nation and globally. This new soundtrack of birdsong plays on but more in the form of a global lament. Although I believe the shared learning of pausing and slowing down expressed here are a living legacy of lockdown, so too is the reality of grief and shared lament. Lament is a biblical song. It is faithful complaint, still believing but bewildered by painful mystery. It is tears put to music or shouted into the wind and it is what we as a world are trying to express in ways probably not shared since the two world wars. So many people right now are trying hard to find the words to their songs of mourning but we are still holding on to each other and my prayer is we still keep singing even when pain is what we share the most.

A BRAND-NEW SONG

'He put a new song in my mouth, a hymn of praise to our God. Many will… put their trust in him.'
Psalm 40:3

He looked like the storybook kind of grandad, with a well-rounded stomach and a mischievous, knowing twinkle in his eye. I first met him when he was serving in the bookshop at a family holiday event with Christian charity Saltmine. He and his wife Val were serving with such joy and care it was clear they saw this as an incredible privilege. His name was Doug Hartman, and I was soon to discover that, in 1981, the *News of the World's* front-page headline described him as 'the king of the conmen'. Yet here he was, serving with such authentic sweetness and humility, it was almost impossible to reconcile the two (apart from the aforementioned mischievous twinkle!).

Doug, in the course of his criminal career, changed the entire banking system in the UK and is the reason that you had to cross a cheque from 1990 onwards! He defrauded the UK banks and post offices out of millions of pounds, charming and scamming his way as he opened mail and cashed every cheque he found that had been sent in the post. Doug had started adult life well, being a driver for war correspondent Richard Dimbleby, but had slowly descended into a gambling habit and engaged in black market selling of watches to meet the increasing hold of his addiction. Further and further into a life of crime he had gone, and many prison spells and new starts had been attempted and failed until he finally found faith and lasting freedom. One judge once described him as 'an evil and dangerous individual incapable of change'. Our meeting that day over the till at Saltmine was the beginning of a wonderful friendship. Doug toured with our theatre company over several years, accompanying us with the production of a play called *Keep Taking the Tablets* written about the Ten Commandments.

At the end of the play Doug would come on and share his story with the prisoners, and they hung on to his every word. For some his heroism lay in his crimes and what he had achieved or pulled off, but when he started to speak there would be tears of recognition and prayers for new hope and new life each time. Doug would always finish with the words from Psalm 103:12: 'As far as the east is from the west, so far has he removed our transgressions from us.' Then he would add: 'My sins are not only forgiven but forgotten by our God.'

Jesus said, 'whoever has been forgiven little loves little' (Luke 7:47), and the opposite was absolutely true for Doug. Until his very last years, Doug drove around to prisons of every kind and category and served in so many ways, with such gratitude and sweetness of spirit, you could see he was overwhelmingly grateful for this new life he had found. Doug had met Jesus through some prison visits and links with Wroxham Road Methodist Church, and God had shown him that through the death and resurrection of Jesus he could be completely free and forgiven. But not only that, he had worked hard to give back. He had even gone around all the banks and post offices he had defrauded to try to ask for forgiveness for all his deception and crime (with mixed responses it's fair to say).

He had deserted his wife Val twice during his years of crime and yet they too were reconciled and remarried. Doug was free not just from prison and crime, but from the shadow of sin and shame over his life. He was forgiven and he knew it. In his latter years one of his best friends was the very chief constable, Peter Barnes, who had chased and arrested Doug many times in the course of his distinguished career in the Norfolk police. Peter, a very strong, loving Christian, forgave Doug completely and offered him friendship and unconditional forgiveness.

Doug's 'song' over all his listeners, and over us today, would be one of hope and the possibility for true freedom and lasting change.

One very noticeable and memorable thing about Doug was that he had managed not only to accept forgiveness, but he had truly forgiven himself, something that in my experience, as a pastor, is rarer and more important than we might think. The reason for Doug's choice of his favourite verse about God forgiving and forgetting was because, somehow, he knew it to be true!

In the Bible, in the Gospel of Luke, the story of Zacchaeus is one that mirrors Doug's life story in many ways. He too was a desperate defrauder, criminalised by all around him and infamous for his crimes. He was so short that he knew he would never be able to set eyes on Jesus in the crowd, yet, somehow, he too knew that he needed to see Him.

I myself know the pain of trying to see over tall people at festivals and theatres and can well imagine the determination to climb a tree so as not to miss out (I have spent many concerts and festivals on the shoulders of others!).

Jesus sees Zacchaeus in the crowd and says He would like to come and stay and eat with him straight away. A little bit forward of Jesus by today's standards (we might think), and even slightly presumptuous, but perhaps He does so as He knows how undeserving Zacchaeus will feel. In spite of Zacchaeus' infamy, even maybe because of it, Jesus picks him to eat with out of the whole crowd. I can only imagine what this must have felt like for Zacchaeus, believing he was the least deserving, yet chosen for special honour and even friendship with Jesus.

Zacchaeus' confession comes a bit more suddenly than Doug's, but the desire to change and to accept a brand-new life and heart are the same. Zacchaeus too says he will repay and give money to the poor. He does this, not to *earn* acceptance and forgiveness, but because he *has received it* already. The Christian faith is quite unique in this – we change our life and ways, not to earn this love from Jesus, but because we already have it.

In this story in Luke 19, Jesus ends their meal and conversation together by saying 'For the Son of Man came to seek and save the lost' (verse 10). Zacchaeus may well have been seeking Jesus in the tree but what he hadn't expected was that Jesus was equally seeking him.

As I come to the end of this last chapter, I hope and pray that whatever else you remember from this book, this will stay with you:

There is a new song for you to sing, whether you are stuck, or your song has been silenced, or even stolen.

No matter how stuck or in despair you feel right now, God does offer you a song of joy and forgiveness, one of grace and a total fresh start, like Doug and Zacchaeus.

The bird, our eponymous hero of this book if you like, may have stopped singing, but this is only temporary. The choice to rediscover your song lies within you. Zacchaeus had to climb a tree, and we too might have to take action to show Jesus that we are seeking Him as He is seeking us.

All our notes of fallenness and shame can and will strengthen the new song that God will give us to sing; in the powerful hands of a redeeming God, our song can even help others to find their song of hope, in harmony and resonance with ours. We can expect and accept total forgiveness, and, like Doug, we too can live completely transformed lives from that place of freedom and grace.

> Amazing grace! How sweet the sound
> That saved a wretch like me!
> I once was lost, but now am found;
> Was blind, but now I see.
>
> 'Twas grace that taught my heart to fear,
> And grace my fears relieved;
> How precious did that grace appear
> The hour I first believed.
> (John Newton[4])

Epilogue

Dear reader, my heart in writing this book has been to encourage you whether you are new to faith, haven't yet found faith, whether you are stuck, or whether you feel you have yet to discover your song. God loves you. We even read in the Old Testament that He sings over your life, like a mother over her young child (see Zephaniah 3:17).

May you find your own voice, your vocation, may you use your voice to speak up for justice, for faith, for the beautiful value of every human being on God's earth, for the poor, for the rescue of the planet and may you always have your song renewed and refreshed by the amazing truth that you are loved and forgiven as a daily reality, thanks to the death and resurrection of Jesus.

It sounds like a reason to sing to me!

My life goes on an endless song,
above earth's lamentations.
I catch the sweet, though far-off hymn
That hails a new creation...

Since Love is Lord of heaven and earth,
how can I keep from singing?
(Robert Lowry, based on Psalm 145[5])

ENDNOTES

[1] C.S. Lewis, 'A word about *praising*', in *Reflections on the Psalms* (Glasgow: HarperCollins, 2017).

[2] 'WHO urges more investments, services for mental health', taken from www.who.int [Accessed 14 May 2021].

[3] William Henry Davies, 'Leisure', (1911).

[4] John Newton, *Amazing Grace*, (1772).

[5] Robert Lowry, *How Can I Keep from Singing*, (1868).

With special thanks to:

Val Egan for her wonderful initial proof-reading.

Michelle Worthington for being such a great writing buddy on our Cafe Thursdays.

For Jeff Lucas for his lovely forward and ongoing encouragement. Cathy Madavan, Jill Garrett and Searchlight theatre company for their lovely recommendations.

For Micha Jazz and the whole wonderful team at Waverley Abbey Trust for believing in and catching the vision for this second book.

For Kate and Yasmin for being wonderful editors and to Michele, Jonny, Janette, Ant and Joy for the brilliant design and production work.

Other titles from Judy Moore

The Dog Who Thought His Name Was No

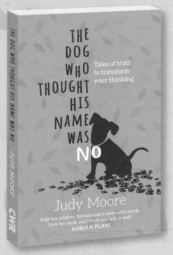

ISBN: 978-1-78259-751-3

Judy has experienced some drama in her life...

These experiences have taught her some key truths – particularly about the way we view ourselves and God. Just like the dog who heard the word 'No' so often he thought it was his name, the words we hear directed at us can shape our identity and influence our beliefs.

Judy shares her stories and invites you to explore, in a humorous yet profound way, how you can tune into God's voice and let Him transform your thinking.

'Judy's words come from the heart and sparkle with warmth, wit and wisdom.'

JEFF LUCAS

waverleyabbeyresources.org

WAVERLEY ABBEY TRUST

We are a charity serving Christians around the world with practical resources and teaching. We support you to grow in your Christian faith, understand the times in which we live, and serve God in every sphere of life.

waverleyabbeycollege.ac.uk

waverleyabbeyresources.org

waverleyabbeyhouse.org